SHORT TALES
Fables

The Fox and the Grapes

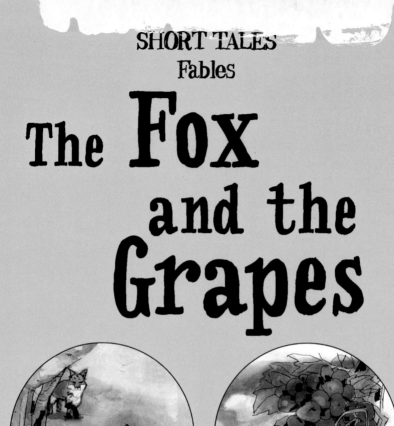

Adapted by Christopher E. Long
Illustrated by John Cboins

WAYLAND

First published in 2014 by Wayland

Copyright © 2014 Wayland

Wayland
338 Euston Road
London NW1 3BH

Wayland Australia
Level 17/207 Kent Street
Sydney, NSW 2000

Adapted Text by Christopher E. Long
Illustrations by John Cboins
Colours by John Cboins
Edited by Stephanie Hedlund
Interior Layout by Kristen Fitzner Denton and Alyssa Peacock
Book Design and Packaging by Shannon Eric Denton
Cover Design by Alyssa Peacock

Copyright © 2008 by Abdo Consulting Group

A cataloguing record for this title is available at the British Library.
Dewey number: 398.2'452-dc23

Printed in China

ISBN: 978 0 7502 7832 4

Wayland is a division of Hachette Children's Books, an Hachette UK company.
www.hachette.co.uk

Fox slept in the cool shade.

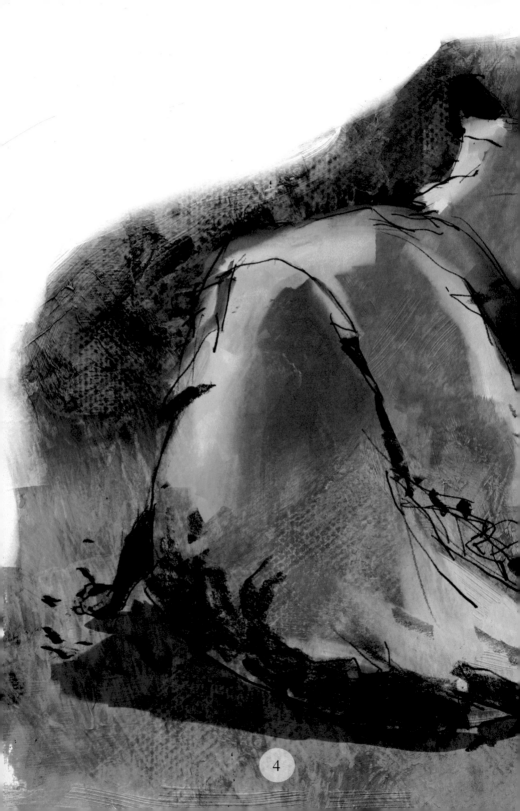

'Fox, you should go and find some lunch' said his mother.

5

'Someone will bring me something to eat' Fox said.

'But your brother is finding his own food' said his mother.

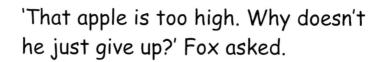

'That apple is too high. Why doesn't he just give up?' Fox asked.

'Because nothing is sweeter than something you have to work to get' his mother said.

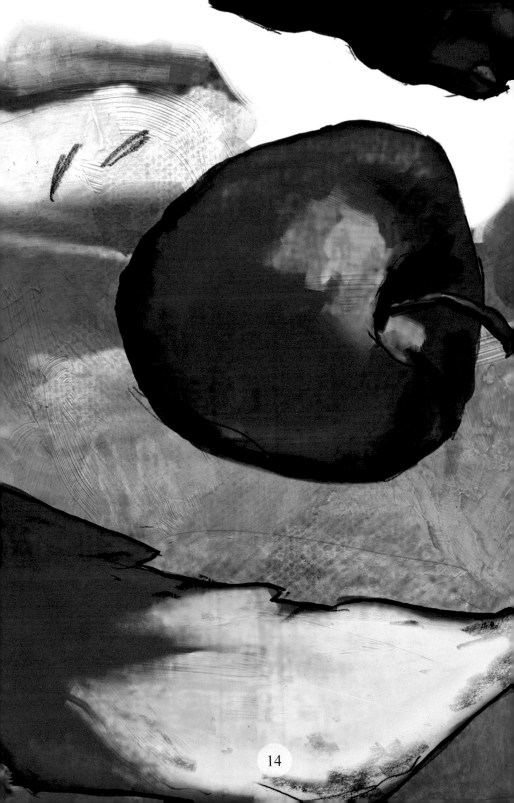

Fox did not understand
what his mother meant.

'Brother Fox, have you had lunch?' Fox's brother asked.

'No, I haven't' Fox said.

'Take my apple' Fox's brother said.

Fox had known someone would
bring him something to eat.

Later that day, Fox got hungry.

He walked into the forest to find his family.

'Those grapes look good' Fox said.

Fox jumped high, but he could not reach the grapes.

'I bet those grapes are sour anyway'
Fox said.

The moral of the story is:

It's easy to despise what you cannot have.